HEART
TO
HEART

HEART TO HEART

Meeting with God in the Lord's Prayer

RACHEL STARR THOMSON

Heart to Heart: Meeting With
God in the Lord's Prayer

Published by Little Dozen Press
Windsor, Ontario, Canada
http://www.littledozen.com

Copyright © 2007 by Rachel Starr Thomson

Visit the author at:
http://rachelstarrthomson.blogspot.com

Unless otherwise noted, Scripture quotations are taken from the King James Version of the Bible. Scripture references marked NIV are taken from the HOLY BIBLE, NEW INTERNATIONAL VERSION®. Copyright © 1973, 1978, 1984 International Bible Society. Used by permission of Zondervan. All rights reserved.

All rights reserved. No part of this publication may be reproduced, stored in a retrieval system, or transmitted, to any form or by any means, electronic, mechanical, photocopying, recording, or otherwise, without the prior written permission of the author.

ISBN: 978-0-9739591-5-4

*This book is affectionately dedicated to
the memory of my grandmother,*

Lois Jean Thomson,

and to her daughter,

Lois Starr,

who reminds me so much of her mother.

TABLE OF CONTENTS

"Lord, teach us to pray..."

Introduction............................i
Our Father.............................1
Father in Heaven....................11
Hallowed Be Thy Name.............19
Thy Kingdom Come................25
Thy Will Be Done 33
Give Us This Day 45
As We Forgive, Forgive Us 55
Deliver Us From Evil 63
Thine Is..............................71

INTRODUCTION

*Jesus' followers once
came to Him with this request:
"Lord, teach us to pray."*

He answered them with a seemingly simple prayer, an approach to God that combined worship, surrender, and the deepest petitions of the human heart, all in the context of a revolutionary relationship with the Father. It is a prayer that approaches the heart of God, for that is what Jesus wanted His followers to do.

A few years ago I found myself making the same request, and there in Matthew's gospel was my answer. I resisted it for a while. Praying by rote, I thought, was "vain repetition"—something Jesus spoke against. Besides, it was cheating.

Nevertheless, stymied by Jesus' very clear instruction ("when you pray, say..."),

I laid my foolish notions down and began to do as He had said. I did not dream what riches were to be found by doing so. For the Lord's Prayer is far more than rote or ritual. It is not a magic formula whereby we can manipulate God or better ourselves. Rather, it is the prayer of a Son who knew His Father well, and desired that we should know Him.

Paul spoke to the church in Ephesus of "the unsearchable riches of Christ."[1] Not least among those riches are the marvelous insights Jesus gives us into His Father's heart. In the pride and delight of kinship, Jesus brings us before the throne and bids us know the Eternal One who would have us for His children. This book is my testimony to some of those riches: to the things I have learned about my Father and the profound joy and confidence to be found in them. I pray that it will bless you, and that the Spirit of Christ may catch you up to the heart of the One who gives life meaning and sanctity, fulfills our needs, promises a kingdom, and teaches us to call Him "Father."

---

[1] Ephesians 3:8

Father!

I would I were a child,
That I might look, and laugh, and say, My Father!
And follow Thee with running feet, or rather
Be led thus through the wild.

How I would hold thy hand!
My glad eyes often to thy glory lifting,
Which casts all beauteous shadows, ever shifting,
Over this sea and land.

If a dark thing came near,
I would but creep within thy mantle's folding,
Shut my eyes close, thy hand yet faster holding,
And so forget my fear.

O soul, O soul, rejoice!
Thou art God's child indeed, for all thy sinning;
A trembling child, yet his, and worth the winning
With gentle eyes and voice.

The words like echoes flow.
They are too good; mine I can call them never...
And yet He said it so;
'Twas He who taught our child-lips to say, Father!

Father! I dare at length.
My childhood, thy gift, all my claim in speaking;
Sinful, yet hoping, I to Thee come, seeking
Thy tenderness, my strength.

GEORGE MACDONALD,
from the poem *I Would I Were a Child*.

OUR FATHER

*After this manner therefore
pray ye: Our Father...*

Once, a very long time ago, there was a garden.

Six days of uproarious joy created it.

Out of darkness came a Voice, and then light, galaxies spinning, earth and water, wings and running feet — life. There was nothing, and then there was colour: green trees, blue seas, shimmering grey mists. And a garden.

Then the One to whom the Voice belonged stooped down and made something with His hands. He "formed man of the dust of the ground, and breathed into his nostrils the breath of life; and man became a living soul."[1]

There was life before Adam, but the dust-man had something the other living creatures did not have. He was a living soul. Somehow his existence, his being, reflected the Being of his Creator. The Living God and the Living Soul fellowshipped together in the garden. They walked together in the cool of the day. Their relationship was the heartbeat of Eden.

I wonder what Adam called God. When he opened his eyes and knew that the Creator was, what did he call him?

Names play a big part in the Genesis story. God named Adam. Adam named Eve and all the animals. Names are important because they put us into relationship with those around us. I dislike name tags, because I think if someone wants to know my name he ought to take the trouble to ask for it, and so create a relationship between us. What I call someone — mother, father, judge, officer, first name, pet name — determines who he is to me and who I am to him.

We don't know what Adam called God. That is because the day came when the heartbeat of Eden stopped, when the relationship was severed, and Adam, once called a Living Soul, began to die.

Generations later, people had not only

---
[1] Genesis 2:7

forgotten God's name. By and large, they had forgotten He even existed.

∞

"Now the Lord said unto Abram, Get thee out of thy country, and from thy kindred, and from thy father's house unto a land that I will shew thee: And I will make of thee a great nation, and I will bless thee, and make thy name great; and thou shalt be a blessing: And I will bless them that bless thee, and curse him that curseth thee: and in thee shall all families of the earth be blessed."[2]

And so a new chapter began. God began the process that would one day restore Eden.

Abram called God "Lord." It sounds natural to us, but it didn't to Abram's contemporaries. "Lord." Lord of what? The nations of the world had lords for everything. One lord for the Nile, one lord for the farm, one lord for the city, one lord for the house; lords and gods galore. Their gods all had names to connect them to their specific role, their specific place of lordship. And here were Abram and his descendants running around referring to "Lord" and "God."

Four hundred years after Abram had become Abraham—"Father of Many"—one

---
Genesis 12:1-3

of the Many approached a burning bush and saw God there. In that moment something in him reached out to know who this God of Abraham was.

"And Moses said unto God, Behold, when I come unto the children of Israel, and shall say unto them, The God of your fathers hath sent me unto you; and they shall say to me, What is his name? What shall I say unto them? And God said unto Moses, I AM THAT I AM: and he said, Thus shalt thou say unto the children of Israel, I AM hath sent me unto you."[3]

If Moses had hoped to pin God down and put Him in a glass case with a neat label underneath, his hopes were shattered. "I AM THAT I AM." Such a name takes God outside of this world's limitations, outside of our whole sphere of reference. Only the Creator, the Voice from the garden, could possess such a name.

The name given to Moses is often translated as "Yahweh" or "Jehovah." Throughout the Old Testament, it is indicated by spelling "LORD" in capital letters. He is the awe-inspiring Adoshem, "Lord of the Name." Because they do not wish to take the name of the Lord in vain, Orthodox Jews often refer to God simply as Hashem—"The Name."

---

[3] Exodus 3:13-14

∾

A cluster of men sat around their leader, a man with rough hands and an unsophisticated northern accent. "Lord," they asked, "teach us to pray."

And He said, "After this manner pray ye: Our Father which art in heaven..."[4]

Jesus of Nazareth had a way of using unexpected words to turn a discussion of the ordinary on its head. For example: "Father."

He called Hashem "Father."

Our Father.

With one word, the carpenter placed us into a new relationship with God. Not the relationship of subject to king, of prisoner to judge, or even of dust to Creator. He put us into the relationship of child to father.

This changes everything.

I pray, "Give me bread." And I need not come with my head bowed to the dirt, groveling, begging. I need not come with something to trade, some price to pay that I may eat. God is my Father, and "what man is there of you, whom if his son ask bread, will he give him a stone? Or if he ask a fish, will he give him a serpent? If ye then, being

---
Matthew 6:9

evil, know how to give good gifts unto your children, how much more shall your Father which is in heaven give good things to them that ask him?"[5]

I pray, "Forgive my debts." And though I come smelling like pigs and filthy from time spent wallowing in the world's muck, I do not ask forgiveness of a judge who sits high above me in anger and malice. I ask it of a father who is watching for me, as Jesus said in the story of the Prodigal Son: "But when he was yet a great way off, his father saw him, and had compassion, and ran, and fell on his neck, and kissed him."[6]

Welcome, child. Welcome to the garden.

"Thy kingdom come." Revive the heartbeat. Walk with God again.

For nearly two years when I was a teenager, my parents went away almost every weekend to work at trade shows, while I stayed home and babysat the youngest six children. We had a perfectly nice time at home without them. But when I would go to bed at night, I was never entirely at peace. No matter how well I handled the household or how much fun we had, I could not truly breathe easily until they were home again.

Even so, we do not have peace until

---
5 Matthew 7:9-11
6 Luke 15:20

Abba comes home.

Jesus rarely used any word but "Father" to describe God. Well; and He had the right. He is the only begotten Son of God, is He not? As I write this, I have a disquieted feeling that I may be on dangerous ground. God is a judge, a king, a Creator. I don't wish to encourage irreverence for Him. Maybe I am wrong to say that He is our loving Father.

Maybe there is a Father, there is a Son, and there are millions of little minions (us).

The truth is, I can hardly believe it myself. I am still trying that word on for size: "Father." Our Father.

Once—also a long time ago, but not so long as before—there was another garden. A woman stood in it, weeping. She had loved a man and placed all of her hope in him, and he was dead. Now his body had been stolen and every last shred of dignity denied him.

"Woman," a voice said, "why weepest thou?"

She turned, and through her tears saw a man approaching. A gardener, in all probability.

"Sir," she said, "if thou hast borne him hence, tell me where thou hast laid him, and

I will take him away."

(Dear Mary Magdalene — if she could have lifted Jesus' broken body alone and carried Him away somewhere safe, I think she would have done it.)

He said, "Mary."

And she knew.

"Rabboni," she cried, "Master."

"Jesus saith unto her, Touch me not; for I am not yet ascended to my Father: but go to my brethren, and say unto them, I ascend unto my Father, and your Father; and to my God, and your God."[7]

"But when ye pray, use not vain repetitions, as the heathen do: for they think that they shall be heard for their much speaking. Be not ye therefore like unto them: for your Father knoweth what things ye have need of, before ye ask him. After this manner therefore pray ye:

"Our Father, which art in heaven..."

Welcome, child, to the garden.

Thy kingdom come.

---

[7] John 20:14-17

Something More

"I know this earth is not my sphere,
For I cannot so narrow me but that
I still exceed it."

ROBERT BROWNING

When, with all the loved around thee,
Still, thy heart says, "I am lonely,"
It is well; the truth hath found thee.
Rest is with the Father only.

GEORGE MACDONALD

FATHER IN HEAVEN

Our Father which art in heaven...

There are words that call up visions from the depths of who we are, words that haunt us and call to us. There are words that are bigger than themselves, that point to something indefinable. For me, "home" is one of those words.

When I was very young I used to make up stories about a home. It didn't have a name then. When I grew a little older, I called it Haven House. It was a big, ramshackle old building with an orchard behind it and a loft where children slept in beds made of straw. An elderly couple owned it. There were somewhere between six and twenty children and young people living with them—orphans, mostly, and poor persecuted street children.

They all had names like Faith and Peace and Justice and Thankful. Their worldly goods were few. Every day the older ones went out to work for food. Their clothes were patched and the roof probably leaked. But they had love, and that in wagon loads.

I'm not sure why I dreamed up Haven House. I suspect it arose in my imagination during a night spent dwelling on images from *Oliver Twist* and *Pilgrim's Progress*. Whether or not this is the case, it tapped into a part of me that has never truly been at home.

Does that sound like an ungrateful thing to say? As a child I was surrounded by people who loved me. I still am. I have parents who are still together, eleven younger brothers and sisters, true friends and loving relatives. And I am grateful for them. Yet I'm not at home, even with them.

Maybe my sense of estrangement comes from our lack of a place to call home. In the last half of my life, moves have nearly outnumbered years. We've gone from Ontario, Canada, to California to Michigan to Canada again; and from house to house to house within those locations. We've changed churches, changed work, changed furniture, and anything else we could change. The lack of roots has been frustrating at best, crippling at worst. Through the years I've often quoted the verse in Hebrews that reads, "For here we have no continuing city, but we seek one to come."[1]

Often I've thought that I would feel settled if we could just move in somewhere and never leave again. When that word "home" comes to haunt me, I imagine a big house in the country with trees and flower gardens that I can make my resting place. I imagine getting married someday and having children and raising them in one spot. I still think I'd like that. When I'm old I think I'd like to look at the wall and see the marks where we measured the children as they grew. I think I'd like to have my grandchildren run barefoot across the same lawn where my children played; across the same yard where I ran barefoot, when I was young and still did things like that. But I've come to realize that even if all of these dreams came true, the word "home" would still haunt me.

Why?

"Home" means childhood. "Home" means love. "Home" means a future in a familiar place. "Home" means permanence.

"Home" is not to be found on Earth.

Remember what the first European settlers in America called themselves? We talk about them every year come harvest time, but we forget what they knew. We forget

---

1   Hebrews 13:14

why they called themselves "Pilgrims."

Today, if you go to the heartland of America, you can find whole counties where people live the way their ancestors did a hundred years ago. They are the Amish. They live here. They work here. They raise children, laugh, and die here. But if you hear the word "America," you probably won't think of them. They live here, but they don't really belong.

Since America's founding in the eighteenth century, thousands of immigrants have made this land their home. They've settled in, bringing with them other languages, other cultures, other ways of life. The joy of starting over is mingled with fond remembrance of "the old country." My own ancestors were immigrants. Chances are yours were, too. And somehow that love of the old country never really goes away. I'm about half Scottish, and like most members of the Scots diaspora, I would love to make my way north to the island where my ancestors were born. When I hear bagpipes or see pictures of the Highlands, something jumps inside of me. It's strange that it's so. I've never been to Scotland. I don't know anyone there. And yet part of me still remembers it.

Have I touched a nerve in your own heart yet? Have you found the part of you that isn't at home? I hope so. Because I have wonderful, glorious news. The dream of home is not just a fantasy. We have a home. Jesus pointed to it when He prayed, "Our Father, which art in Heaven."

Home is where my Father is; home is in Heaven! Everything around us is temporary. Every day I live as a Christian is a day that takes me nearer the home for which I long. It is a day closer to perfect love, to the permanence that comes from living in the light of the Beginning and the End. Everything I have ever longed for is there, in Heaven.

As I've grown older, my sense of being away from home has deepened. And even as I try to settle here, on the soil of this Earth—because this is what God has called me to do—I realize that I am still a pilgrim. I am like the Amish who settled in America but retained an identity that is not American.

As the world around grows increasingly wicked, I am grateful that this is not my home. As politics and philosophies whirl around my head like a cloud of gnats, I smile inside to know that it will all pass away, and I'll find my feet still on the road to home. As I pass through this world, I pray that others will see that I breathe the air of another country, and will join me on the road. How I wish that someday we will all go home.

I have one last thing to say in regard to the words "home" and "Heaven." Too often

Heaven has been painted as a place where we will float around, unconnected from anything that moved us on Earth—anything that made us laugh, or cry, or sleep in perfect peace. This is not the case. I believe that everything that home is on earth is only a shadow of its true self in Heaven. When you meditate on the word "home," what comes to you? What moves your heart? I believe you will find it there—not a shadow anymore, but the true thing, in perfection.

Somehow, I wouldn't be surprised to find that our mansions in Heaven are something like the old ramshackle house I dreamed of as a child. And I know that I would be perfectly happy, perfectly at peace there—even if the roof leaked.

Hallowed

I heard the voice of Jesus say, "I am this dark world's Light;

Look unto Me, thy morn shall rise, and all thy days be bright."

I looked to Jesus, and I found in Him my Star, my Sun;

And in that light of life I'll walk, till traveling days are done.

HORATIUS BONAR,
from "I Heard the Voice of Jesus Say"

HALLOWED BE THY NAME

*Our Father
which art in heaven,
Hallowed be thy name.*

Some time ago I attended an expo with my sisters and my parents.

We were advertising our ability to make music together in hopes that someone would pay us to do so. Several hundred other people with other skills — magicians, singers, display builders, lemonade makers — were doing the same. There was nothing remarkable about the gathering, but by the end of the first day something had happened to me. I had become world-weary.

It wasn't the first time. I remember leaving a movie theater after seeing a teen flick that was meant to be funny, heart-sore because of the things I saw and heard around me. Sickened by contact with a world without hope. There have been plenty of other times. I sit and listen and watch, and the vanity of it all becomes overwhelming.

That night my sister and I went up to our hotel room as the day's events closed. There was a painting on the wall. At first glance it seemed to be a picture of desert mountains, much like those I had lived among in California. A bit of home. But as we looked, the picture began to change. There were faces in it. Dozens of them. Evil, leering faces. We stared in fascination until we had found them all: thirty or so, if I remember correctly.

I didn't sleep peacefully that night. The mountains in the painting were ruined — even nature was corrupted. That night, as on many other nights, I wondered: is there anything holy left in the world?

And then I remember Jesus sitting with His disciples, teaching them to pray. Looking up from a dark world — a world suffocating under a cloak of darkness — looking up, eyes sweeping the heavens, and then smiling, because they have found a window into the Kingdom of Light. "Hallowed be thy name."

He is holy, therefore we are not lost. Beauty exists. Purity exists. Love exists. Goodness exists. All of these things are true because God exists. The unchanging God, the Maker, is holy.

We forget, in the busyness of life, how important that is. Petty things demand all of our attention. Thousands of little voices scream at us, "Look at me, focus on me, give give give to me!" The worst of them all is our own voice. And if we let them, they'll drag us down until the darkness closes over us. It is then, choked by our own selfishness and smeared with the world's blackness, that we need to look up and open our own window into the Kingdom. It is then that we need to hallow Him. To remember who He is. To remember that He is holy.

Yesterday, I read in Isaiah a description of a nation spoiled by its own rebelliousness, where "all joy is darkened, the mirth of the land is gone. In the city is left desolation, and the gate is smitten with destruction." But then there comes a turning point, a moment when, bereft of all that has given meaning to their lives, the people remember to look up and hallow God. "They shall lift up their voice," Isaiah says, "they shall sing for the majesty of the LORD, they shall cry aloud from the sea... from the uttermost part of the earth have we heard songs, even glory to the righteous."[1]

There have been times in my life when everything seemed empty. Relationships

---

[1] Isaiah 24:12, 14, 16

had gone off course; church was a whitewashed tomb; everything I did was a filthy rag. In those times God has reminded me to look to Him, and I have found that I have a reason to sing. I will sing for the majesty of the Lord. I watch relationships ruined by selfishness and think that love is a myth, and then I think on Jesus and know that it is not—He loves me. He loves you. He loves, more purely and truly than any one of us could possibly imagine. I look on the mountains and see the scars left by human beings who can't help tainting everything they touch, and think that beauty isn't real. And then I think on the Creator and remember that the Heart of Beauty still beats. He is still creating.

I have hope, I have joy. He is changing me into His image. I am moving "from glory to glory, even as by the Spirit of the Lord."[2] One day I will be holy, as He is holy.

As I get my eyes upward, past the darkness to the God who still reigns on high, His character begins to work in my life and counteract the darkness. And so I have witnessed holiness here on earth. In the love between a man and woman at the altar. In my baby sister's face as she sleeps. In the movements of a dancer and the strains of a song. In grief and in comfort. The sacred has come into the

---

[2] II Corinthians 3:18

common things of life, and the words of Isaiah are true for me today: "The people that walked in darkness have seen a great light: they that dwell in the land of the shadow of death, upon them hath the light shined."[3]

We live in a culture of irreverence. The names and titles of God are tossed around, even by Christians, as expressions of frustration and anger. Everything beautiful is profaned. But mankind cannot change God. Though we twist every gift He gives us, we cannot change Him. True, we can deface His image in the minds of others. But that does not change who He is.

"Hallowed be thy name." In Jesus' prayer, these words are wings. They are meant to carry us beyond ourselves, beyond this world, beyond everything that holds us down. Look to God, for He is holy.

---

[3] Isaiah 9:2

Reality

"I want to live in the light of the thought of His coming, His triumph — the end of this present darkness, the glory of His seen Presence. This bathes the present in radiance. You won't be sorry then that you trusted when you couldn't see, when neither sun nor stars in many days appeared and no small tempest lay on you. No, you won't be sorry then. So I won't be sorry now. I am believing. 'All joy and peace in believing': the words ring like a chime of bells."

AMY CARMICHAEL,
from *Candles in the Dark*

THY KINGDOM COME

"I saw in the night visions, and, behold, one like the Son of man came with the clouds of heaven, and came to the Ancient of days, and they brought him near before him.

"And there was given him dominion, and glory, and a kingdom, that all people, nations, and languages, should serve him: his dominion is an everlasting dominion, which shall not pass away, and his kingdom that which shall not pass away."

DANIEL 7:13-14

"The kingdom of God is within you."
LUKE 17:2

Sometimes I think it's most tangible in the city.

Walk down the street—past the nightclubs and the tattoo parlours, past the glitz of a five-star hotel or the mundanity of a corner store. You can feel it, a strange oppression and vanity in the air. Go where people are, and look into their faces, and you know, somehow, that we're living on the other side of Eden—and it's dangerous here. Having chased the light out of our world, we're living in a kingdom of darkness. We can't see, or understand; and God knows we're helpless to find a way out.

Living as we do in a material world, it's easy to forget the spiritual reality behind what we see. Yet, walk down the street and you may catch a glimpse. It can be overwhelming to realize how thick the darkness has grown, but don't despair: it isn't the whole story.

For as you walk down the street, you might turn into a house, or a storefront, or perhaps a little church. And here again, you may look into the faces that greet you, but here you see something other than darkness. Something is stirring within these people. There is light in their eyes. Their hearts are awakening to truth.

The kingdom of God has come to them.

God knows we're helpless to find a way out: and He, who walked with us once in the Garden, cares. As Jesus once told a midnight visitor, "God so loved the world, that he gave his only begotten Son, that whosoever believeth on him should not perish, but have everlasting life."[1]

In love for us, God has launched an invasion.

The prophet Daniel once witnessed an awe inspiring gift-giving, as the Ancient of Days, God the Father, presented "one like the Son of man" with an everlasting kingdom, which would reign over all the earth. God gifted His Son with a perishing world. It was a gift of love, both to Christ and to us, for Jesus, Saviour to the core, acting on His Father's behalf, entered the world to plant His kingdom in the soil of rescued hearts. "For God sent not his Son into the world to condemn the world; but that the world through him might be saved."[2]

So it was that John the Baptist, foretold prophet of the LORD, cried, "Repent, for the kingdom of God is at hand!" So it was that Jesus, when first He embarked on His ministry, said, "The time is fulfilled, and the kingdom of God is at hand: repent ye, and believe the gospel."[3] Jesus did not come

---
1 John 3:16
2 John 3:17
3 Mark 1:15

simply as a good man to live an exemplary life, or as a teacher to show people truths about God and themselves—though He did these things, as no other has before or since. Nor did He come merely as a Saviour to set people free from their bonds to live as they please. No, Jesus Christ came into the world as a king entering into His kingdom. He came to claim what was rightfully His: the heart of every man and woman who will own Him as Lord.

He did it sublimely, as we could not have imagined He would do it! He commands our allegiance by washing our feet; demands our worship by humbling Himself. As the terrible thresher of prophecy, He separates the wheat from the chaff: by taking the blows upon Himself, and letting the wheat cling to His scarred hands while the chaff turn their faces and go their own way, into the fire.

Into our guilty world the kingdom of God came in the person of its King, with forgiveness freely offered. Into our corrosion came healing and life. Into our darkness, light. But there is in all of this a terrible condemnation for those who will not bow their knees: "This is the condemnation, that light is come into the world, and men loved darkness rather than light, because their deeds were evil."[4]

Any view of Christianity as fire insurance or a feel-good morality tale is missing the reality of the kingdom. The kingdom of God is that place wherein God has His unhindered rule, and that place is in our hearts. "The kingdom of God is within you," Jesus told a listening crowd. And to live in accordance with His kingdom necessitates a total change of life. "Repent," Jesus told the people of Galilee, "and believe the gospel." Belief in the good news of the king's arrival in our world goes hand in hand with repentance: with a complete about-face in our way of being, an absolute surrender to God's rule and reign.

The fact is, the kingdom of God runs totally counter to anything we have learned growing up in the world. Jesus, the Servant-King, is the heart and center of His realm, and His character defines its laws and principles. There is no room in the kingdom for our self-serving games, our divisions and petty offenses. The King is love, and oneness, and grace. In the world, we preserved ourselves by fear and cunning; Jesus calls us to trust and childlikeness. In the world, we value possessions and position; in the kingdom, we value people and poverty of spirit.

Jesus told His disciples that the king-

---
[4] John 3:19

dom of God was like a grain of yeast, or a mustard-seed: it begins as a very small thing, and grows until it has transformed everything it touches, or become a mighty tree. Historically, the picture is uncanny. The kingdom entered the world in the person of a child born to a virgin. He lived a relatively short life, and died without the earth's most powerful men even knowing He had existed—though, two thousand years later, He can be seen to have had the most profound impact on the culture and history of the world of any man at any time. And though God raised Him from the dead, He did not claim His kingdom in a blaze of military glory. Instead, He left: returned to the Father, where He intercedes for us. But He did not leave us empty-handed. He left us the kingdom.

In a sense, we who have repented and believed the gospel are outposts of heaven. We are a new and living world within an old and dying one. It is ours to walk in the light, to live as children of the day, to worship the True King and oppose the rebellious stewards who have tried to claim this realm for their own. To the darkness, we are the worst sort of traitors, because we dare to live eternal lives while the world tumbles ever nearer its ultimate destruction. The Bible speaks truly when it says that we are at enmity with the world. But at the same time, we are the world's hope: because we have not just been left here to while away the hours until Christ returns. Rather, we have been left here as colonists with a mission: to preach, as Jesus and His disciples did, that the kingdom of God has come, and that if we will surrender ourselves to the King, God has promised to "deliver us from the power of darkness, and translate us into the kingdom of his dear Son."[5]

And so we pray. We pray, for the oppression in the air must be lifted. We pray, for the faces marred by hopelessness and sin. We pray, for the places in our own souls that have yet to kneel before the Merciful Thresher, that have yet to be changed by the yeast of the kingdom.

We pray: "Thy kingdom come."

---

5   Colossians 1:13

Trust

"Why dost thou worry thyself? What use can thy fretting serve? Thou art on board a vessel which thou couldst not steer even if the great Captain put thee at the helm, of which thou couldst not so much as reef a sail, yet thou worriest as if thou wert captain and helmsman. Oh, be quiet; God is master!"

CHARLES H. SPURGEON

THY WILL BE DONE

*Thy will be done in earth,
as it is in heaven.*

God loves you, and has a wonderful plan for your life.

How many times have you heard that said, in one way or another? We love to quote Jeremiah 29:11, where God says, "'I know the plans I have for you,' declares the LORD, 'plans to prosper you and not harm you, plans to give you hope and a future'" (NIV). In our churches we talk a lot about doing God's will in our lives, but first it seems we have to find it. How many times have you heard that phrase? "I'm trying to find God's will for my life." And this, apparently, is tricky. Of course we have the Bible to tell us what God's will for us is. The trouble is, the Bible is so... so... well, it's so much like the Bible, as opposed to being like MapQuest: and this is what many of us really want. We want something to tell us point by point, step by step, from beginning to end, not only where we're going but also how we're going to get there.

Many times in my life I've gotten on my knees and asked God to show me His will for my life. It sounds good and pious, but the truth is, much of the time I'm just looking for guarantees. I want God to take all the uncertainty out of life and make it easy. He never does. For my own good He chooses to leave the future shrouded in mystery. I want to know where I'll be tomorrow, but my Father wants me to get up and walk today.

The world has a love/hate relationship with the idea of destiny. On the one hand they hate being told that they aren't in complete control of their own lives. On the other hand they know they're not; and destiny is a wonderful idea because it gives them some hope that life isn't just spinning wildly out of control for no reason, and someday, somehow, their lives will mean something significant.

As Christians there are two things we need to remember: we have a known destiny, and we follow a loving God.

I have no desire to spark a doctrinal debate. I don't feel a need to discuss free will versus predestination or to set Calvin and Arminius at each other's throats again. These things "are too high for me" and I don't wish to meddle in them. However, my Bible tells me that I have a destiny. It says so in Romans 8:29, right after it says that all things work together for my good:

"For whom [God] did foreknow, he also did predestinate to be conformed to the image of his Son, that he might be the firstborn among many brethren."

There you have it: destiny. I have a destiny (so do you), and I'm living it out every day. Every day, every moment, every interaction, every circumstance, is another step down a path. I will someday reach the end, and the end is that I will be like Christ. Mark you, I will not become Christ. I'm not looking for a nirvana-like experience that will merge me with the Universe. I won't wake up and discover that I've always existed or that I speak Hebrew or that I've grown a beard. I will still be me, but I will be a new me; I will be like Christ.

I will be a child of God in every sense of the word. I'll be perfect like Christ—my inside and my outside will match up. I will have joy like Christ, I will love like Christ. I will delight fully in God, my All in All. I will have become a true human being with no more temptation to be a human doing. Everything I do will flow naturally from who I am, and everything I am will flow naturally from who God is. I can't really express the incredible freedom contained in this; really, I can't even look it in the face yet. But I'll get there. It's my destiny.

It's so important for us to know this. We should remind ourselves of it every day. Knowing where we're finally headed won't necessarily tell us what to do tomorrow. You can know the will of God—to make you like Christ—and still feel like you haven't "found" it because you don't know where you're going to work or who you're going to marry or what you're going to eat for lunch tomorrow. I understand the feeling, but it's important to remember our finish line, if only because we tend to live what we believe. If we believe we're just running around in circles and we haven't entered God's will for our lives yet, we'll live like it. On the other hand, if we believe that everything that comes into our lives is sent by God for the master purpose of making us like Jesus, we'll live as though it's true. And the marvelous thing is, it is true—and the truth will set us free.

When I sit down to write a novel, I generally have two things: a handful of characters and an ending. Everything else comes later, but I am confident that all of the details will eventually fall into place because

I know where the story's headed. In a sense we are like characters in a story (and we're a lot better off than the characters in my books because we've been shown the ending, whereas I make my characters suffer blindly for hundreds of pages before working it all out in the end). As characters in this story, though, we have another imperative. It is not enough for us to know the end, because we cannot know it with any certainty unless we also know the Author.

Paul tells us that we Christians are literally being "led" through life. In the past our flesh led us around by the nose, but now we "walk not after the flesh, but after the Spirit."[1] We have a guide; we make a decision to follow Him. The trouble is, the Spirit does not always lead us down paths strewn with roses. Every life will face adversity in varying degrees. (No one of us has the right to judge someone else's situation as "easier" or even "harder" than our own. Never scoff at the burden someone else is carrying. Scripture treats pain and suffering in many different ways but it never belittles it.) When we become Christians and leave the kingdom of this world for the Kingdom of God, we enter into a whole new set of trials. For one thing, we make an Enemy—Satan, and he's very real. For another thing, we learn that we have to do a painful thing called "denying

---

1   Romans 8:1, 4

ourselves." Just look at the best examples of following the Spirit. Jesus did it better than anyone and He was crucified.

Do you see why we have to learn who God is in all of this? If God is not good, we're in serious trouble. If He doesn't love us, we might as well keel over and die today. If God is the cruel, heartless tyrant Satan says He is (and Satan is always trying to make God in his own image), then we're all better off bailing out now. I don't know where we should go, but we'd be fools to follow the Spirit one more step.

Paul understood this well. He spent half of Romans 8 talking about being led by the Spirit, and he spent the other half laying out in the strongest terms the heart-wrenchingly powerful love of God for us. The two concepts are threaded together throughout the chapter.

"For as many as are led by the Spirit of God, they are the sons of God. For ye have not received the spirit of bondage again to fear; but ye have received the Spirit of adoption, whereby we cry, Abba, Father. The Spirit itself beareth witness with our spirit, that we are the children of God: And if children, then heirs; heirs of God, and joint-heirs with Christ; if so be that we suffer with him, that we may be also glorified together."[2]

---
[2] Romans 8:14-17

I spent a while meditating on these verses, and wrote this in my journal:

I have learned that if I am "in Christ Jesus," then I have consented to stop walking "after the flesh," in the way that seems normal, safe, and in my best interests, and "walk after the Spirit." And this, I quickly discover, is not always easy. It involves "mortifying the deeds of the body." Moreover, the Spirit has a tendency to lead people smack dab into the middle of suffering. Naturally we often recoil from the whole idea. Being led by the Spirit sounds like a matter of being bound in chains that draw us inexorably toward suffering and death.

...which is why Paul hastens to assure that this is not so. "Ye shall live!" he says. The Spirit is leading you to life. Don't you understand that the Spirit has not made slaves of you, but sons? Your old master Sin was a slave master working you to death, but your new Master is not like that. "Ye have not received the spirit of bondage again"—so don't be afraid. You've entered a family. You've been adopted. Your new Father loves you. He's proven how much He loves you in the cross. He has an inheritance for you. You're not one of those adopted children brought in out of obligation and then overlooked and stepped on; you're no Cinderella. You're a joint-heir with Christ.

If we don't understand that God loves us, we will quail at His will. Jesus didn't go to the cross hoping that His Father would turn out to be loving in the end. He knew the love of God—the passionate, burning, all-encompassing love of God. He embodied it. And therein lies the key to the whole problem. Can we trust the will of God? Can we follow the Spirit without fear? Yes, for one astounding reason—He sent Jesus! In the person of Jesus Christ, in His life and death and life again, the love of God has proven itself. It is perfect love, and it casts out fear, and the heart that truly understands it will fall to its knees and pray, "Thy will be done."

Every one of us is born in slavery. We are sold under sin. We inhabit the same sphere with Satan, who enjoys nothing more than degrading and destroying those who were made in the image of God. Most of us have been hurt in some way by authority figures in our lives. We all have scarred hearts. In the day we come to Christ, we are redeemed from slavery and adopted into the family of God. Death starts working backwards and life is restored to us. A million years from now we will be a million times more alive than we are today. But many of us carry over some pagan ideas from our old life. When God picks up a rod to chastise us, we cringe as though He would destroy us if He could. When we go to Him, we act as if He was a capricious, selfish, hard-to-please tyrant instead of our Abba, our Papa, who sent His beloved Son to die for us. Oh children of God, look at the cross! Look at Jesus! See how much He loves you. Let His perfect love cast out fear.

Look at Jesus. In the gospels, the first time we hear Jesus say, "Thy will be done," He is preaching on a mountain to hundreds of captivated listeners. He is surrounded by friends; He is the Healer, the Provider, the Great Rabbi. The next time we hear Him say it, He is in a garden alone at night; His friends asleep, His enemies coming; He is bleeding, agonized, seized with the vision of His own death. Yet still He says the words, "Not my will, but Thine be done."

For us He did this. He loved and trusted His Father. He submitted to the Spirit who led Him. Together this Great Coalition conspired to rescue us. We were the reward for all of His agony. I was. You were. I asked Him two months ago how much He loved me, and He answered. He said, "I loved you to the cross."

Remember that. Remember that, and nothing in life will overcome you. Yes, you will face trials. The will of God will bring them into your life so that you can be changed and molded and made in His image. But don't forget that God's love guides His hand. Pray this prayer without fear: "Thy will be done, on earth, in me, as it is in heaven. Remember the end of the story: as Paul said, "For I reckon that the sufferings of this present time are not worthy to be compared with the glory which shall be revealed in us."[3] More than that, remember the Author.

God loves you, and has a wonderful plan for your life. Get up and walk with rejoicing.

Longing

O God of truth, for whom alone I sigh,
  Knit thou my heart by strong,
    sweet cords to thee.
I tire of hearing; books my patience try;
  Untired to thee I cry;
  Thyself my all shalt be.

PIERRE CORNEILLE

As the deer pants for streams of water,
so my soul pants for you, O God.
My soul thirsts for God, for the living God.
When can I go and meet with God?

KING DAVID
(Psalm 42:1-2, NIV)

GIVE US THIS DAY

Give us this day our daily bread.

The scene is a desert mountain, an unusually scrubby sort of place to be the center of so much activity. We don't know how many people were there—Matthew, who recorded the event for us, didn't bother to count. He just says "multitudes." Up in the mountain sits a young man with an unusual amount of light in His eyes; around Him are twelve other young men, whose idea of God He is busy demolishing in order to build something far truer in its place—beginning with the monumental words "Our Father."

Some people have the idea that Jesus somehow changed who God was. They think that the God who revealed Himself to Moses amidst clouds and flame in Sinai was a malicious, petty judge with a great love for squashing people, but since Jesus came God somehow transformed Himself into a big softy who doesn't care what we do as long as we can feel good about it. I was browsing in a bookstore recently when I came across a book entitled *God: An Itinerary*. The author's intent was to trace all of the different ways "God" has been perceived throughout history and across cultures. I can't quote it with absolute accuracy since I didn't think the book worth buying, but I remember it said, "The vengeful God of the Hebrews is not the intimate God of the Christians." I think Jesus would have a thing or two to say to that author, because God is who He is, and He does not change. He has not changed. The only things that change are man's ideas about God. Human beings have a penchant for forgetting things and a tendency to make things up to fill the gaps. By the time Jesus physically stepped into the pages of history, the Jews had forgotten a lot and made up a whole lot more. Jesus came to set the record straight. As John the Baptist said of Him, "No man hath seen God at any time; the only begotten Son, which is in the bosom of the Father, he hath declared him."[1]

"Give us this day our daily bread." A simple request. It is the first specific reference to our needs in the Lord's Prayer. God,

---
[1] John 1:8

we need to eat; we recognize that You are the Provider. Please give us bread today. This little prayer tears down one of the biggest misconceptions about God, which millions of people still hold today — the idea that God only cares about our so-called spiritual lives. As far as everything else goes, we're on our own; or maybe, as Buddha would have it, nothing is real and so our "needs" are not needs at all, they're just illusions that make us miserable. We won't be happy until we've learned to stop needing things like bread and water and love.

This is a lot of rot and Jesus made that pretty clear. What kind of father carefully leads devotions with his children every day and then sends them out to scrounge in the streets for their own food? One of the most incredible things about the God Jesus declared — the God all of Scripture bears witness to — is how beautifully unselfish He is. He is a God who cares. He is a God who provides what we need because He loves us. Every god ever created in the image of man has been like man: only concerned for the people insofar as they benefit the god. But God, the real God, I AM THAT I AM, is not like that. He causes the sun to rise on the evil and on the good; He makes rain to fall on the just and on the unjust. He loves those who do not love Him.[2]

---

[2] Matthew 5:45-46

However, because God is who He is and is so infinitely wise and unselfish, He does not give us everything just the way we want it. You see, "Give us this day our daily bread" is not exactly a prayer we would make up. We're far more comfortable praying, "Give us this day a million dollars so we can keep ourselves happy from here on out." Or, at the very least, "Give us this day a steady income and a good pension plan." We want guarantees, and the unchanging character of our Father is not guarantee enough. There was a time, long before Jesus' coming, in which Israel literally had to trust God for daily bread. It was called manna, and it fell out of heaven each morning. God told the Israelites that manna would be there every day for them to go out and collect, but they were not to take any more than they needed for that day. But some of the people decided that God wasn't trustworthy—He was lying, or capricious, or forgetful, or something. So they stocked up on the stuff. In the morning it was rancid and full of worms.

Now, some of you reading this may never have been in a position where you felt it necessary to ask God for your next meal. But if you are truly attempting to follow God, I am quite sure there is something for which you find yourself forced to go to God every day. For example, I pray for love for my family. God has never yet given me a stockpile of it. I have to draw on Him every day if I want to be anything like the loving sister and daughter He wants me to be.

So here's a question: why? Why does God force us into daily dependence on Him? Why doesn't He just give us the stockpile? It seems to me that it would be much easier for me to obey Him if He did. Why doesn't He give me perfect faith and fill my life with all sorts of miracles and constant manifestations of His presence? Why doesn't He let me know what my future holds and give me all the victory over everything NOW?

How long do you think I would stick with Him if He did?

You see, I am not yet the unselfish being God is. How much of the love I think I hold for Him is really only there because I need Him? One of the sweetest things in the world is the love between a mother and her newborn child. That baby doesn't care for anyone as much as it cares for Mama. Why? Because Mama holds it and sings to it and cuddles it and changes it and bathes it and feeds it... and only Mama can do that. A baby's love for its mother has little to do with who that mother is as a person and a lot to do with the baby's needs. That tiny child has not yet developed the character to love apart from need. That will come as the child grows. In the meantime, God made that child extremely needy so that it would stay close to the person it needs the most.

God keeps us in daily dependence on Him so that we will stay close to Him, and the more we cling to Him and learn to trust Him, the more we will grow into His character: His unselfishness, His love. It is not a bad thing for us to need Him so much, nor is it wrong for our love for Him to be based on that need. He doesn't expect an infant to behave like an adult, although He does expect us to grow. He delights in us just as a mother delights in her little one.

There is another facet to this: as a child grows older, it becomes aware that it has needs that transcend the physical. There comes a day in each of our lives when we realize that we need to be loved. Or some deep colour or beautiful strain of music strikes a new place inside of us, and we become aware of longings we didn't know we had. God keeps us near Him, daily dependent on Him for so many little things, because He knows that we have a deeper need we may not even recognize yet. He knows that the truest hunger in us is not for food or water, not for security or happiness, not for beauty or friendship—the truest hunger in each of our lives is for God Himself. And He will keep us near Him until we learn the truth and throw ourselves into His arms crying only, "Teach me to love You. I want You."

Listen to Jesus:

"I am the bread of life: he that cometh to me shall never hunger; and he that believeth on me shall never thirst... Your fathers did eat manna in the wilderness, and are dead. This is the bread which cometh down from heaven, that a man may eat thereof, and not die. Verily, verily, I say unto you, Except ye eat the flesh of the Son of man, and drink his blood, ye have no life in you. Whoso eateth my flesh, and drinketh my blood, hath eternal life; and I will raise him up at the last day. For my flesh is meat indeed, and my blood is drink indeed.

"He that eateth my flesh, and drinketh my blood, dwelleth in me, and I in him. As the living Father hath sent me, and I live by the Father: so he that eateth me, even he shall live by me."[3]

"Give us this day our daily bread." If we believe that God cares about every aspect of our lives, we will ask Him to provide in every area of our lives. To do so is an act of trust. It is to say, "Father, I believe You are as loving and caring and willing to give as You say You are, and so I ask." Again, we ask for daily bread, "give us this day," because we recognize God's wisdom and love in keeping us constantly dependent on Him. There is no magic formula in the way

---

3   John 6:35, 49-50, 53-57

Jesus prayed. He prayed as He did because He knew who His Father was. If we learn to pray the same way, we will find more than our conscious needs being met. We will come to know Him. In time our prayers may change: beyond the infant's crying to be fed, we may find ourselves so much closer to our Father that we can pray as Job did, as Jesus Himself did, "Though He slay me, yet will I trust Him."[4]

Long before the Word became flesh and dwelt among us, God made His highest will known to His people on Mount Sinai: "And thou shalt love the Lord thy God with all thy heart, and with all thy soul, and with all thy might."[5] This is still the greatest commandment, and through His Son God is lifting us up until we can keep it perfectly. In life and love, in prayer and provision, He reveals Himself to us—the One for whom we are hungry; the One who has given Himself so that we may be full.

---

[4] Job 13:15
[5] Deuteronomy 6:5

Song of the Forgiven

My life flows on in endless song;
Above earth's lamentation
I hear the sweet though far off hymn
That hails a new creation:
Through all the tumult and the strife
I hear the music ringing;
It finds an echo in my soul —
How can I keep from singing?

What though my joys and comforts die?
The Lord my Savior liveth;
What though the darkness gather round!
Songs in the night He giveth:
No storm can shake my inmost calm
While to that refuge clinging;
Since Christ is Lord of Heav'n and earth,
How can I keep from singing?

I lift mine eyes; the cloud grows thin;
I see the blue above it;
And day by day this pathway smoothes
Since first I learned to love it:
The peace of Christ makes fresh my heart,
A fountain ever springing:
All things are mine since I am His —
How can I keep from singing?

ROBERT LOWRY,
How Can I Keep From Singing?

AS WE FORGIVE, FORGIVE US

And forgive us our debts, as we forgive our debtors.

"To err is human, to forgive divine." An old saying: one that rolls off our tongues without much thought. Yet these are true words, truer perhaps than most of us have recognized. Forgiveness is divine. God forgives. The whole great heart of God is to forgive. Without His divine forgiveness there would be no one on this earth who could call himself "Christian." Freedom would be all an illusion, because there would be nothing to break the chains with which we have bound ourselves.

When Jesus taught His people to pray to their Father in heaven, He taught them to ask forgiveness: "Forgive us our debts." And He, who loves us and would have us be "partakers of the divine nature, having escaped the corruption that is in the world through lust,"[1] in the same breath gave us a responsibility: "Forgive us our debts, as we forgive our debtors." When the prayer had ended Jesus went back to this subject:

"For if ye forgive men their trespasses, your heavenly Father will also forgive you: But if ye forgive not men their trespasses, neither will your Father forgive your trespasses."[2]

I've heard more than one believer testify that when he first came to Christ, he found himself struggling — but the struggle was not between belief and unbelief, but between forgiveness and resentment. When we come to God for forgiveness, we find that Jesus' words are an almost tangible reality. We must let go of our self-interest; we have to forgive. This struggle does not only come at conversion. Satan is always trying to plant a root of bitterness, and our flesh is always ready to take offense.

Forgiveness is the catalyst of many a great battle between the old reprobate we used to be and the obedient child God is making us. There's nothing mystical about this. When we choose not to forgive, we make a decision to enthrone Self, and Self

---
1   II Peter 1:4
2   Matthew 6:14-15

is not any more willing to share the throne with God than God is to share the throne with Self. To choose against forgiveness is to say that Self's concerns are more important than obedience, and certainly more important than others.

You see, when we become Christians we throw away our old way of life. God's concerns become our concerns. We seek first His Kingdom; we desire to do His will and be changed into His likeness. And the fact is, God's chief concern is for all the others in this world — all the little people who irritate, offend, and hurt us. We can hardly be united with God if we will not forgive those He has forgiven. (Nor can we say that He doesn't understand, He hasn't been provoked and abused as we have — they killed Him and He forgave them.) Furthermore, He does not just forgive them so that He can admire His own magnanimity. He forgives them because He loves them, just as much as He loves you.

Much of the Christian life as Jesus and Paul and others talked about it is a matter of taking God's part toward others, and this nearly always means putting our own part aside. When Jesus told us how to live, when the Holy Spirit inspired Paul and Peter and John to give commands to the Church, they were not bequeathing either a new Law or a bunch of scattered afterthoughts which will make us better than other people. They were showing us how to love. If we will look at all the New Testament instructions in the light of Jesus' new commandment to "Love one another as I have loved you," we will find that, as a dear friend recently wrote me, "Love unites everything both in ourselves and in the body of Christ." Love unites everything; love makes sense of it all. And it is love—true, bloody, Christ-like love—that must come to govern all that we do and all that we are. John tells us that "God is love";[3] he tells us also that "when he shall appear, we shall be like him."[4] One day we will be like Christ. We are on that journey now.

It is Love we are becoming like, and what better way can God have of training us than by opening our lives to people? People, who are so captivating and so frustrating, so stupid and so brilliant, so funny, strange, loving, hateful, vexatious and resplendent. He loved them in the Garden before they rebelled against Him; He has loved them through the tumultuous ages since; He came and laid His life down for them. They are His heart and He will use them to make us like Him.

It must begin with forgiveness. God allows us to be hurt, allows us to be offended, allows us to be wrongfully treated, so that we can learn what it really means to love.

---
3   1 John 4:8
4   1 John 3:2

We may feel a great deal of affection and warmth toward people while they are keeping us happy, but such love is fickle. The great test of it comes when someone trespasses against you: when your child despises you, when your spouse is cruel, when your friend betrays you, when your parent's actions slap you in the face, when your church turns on you. Trespasses can be small or earth-shatteringly large; real or imagined; intentional or hardly even realized. No matter what they are, they always bring us face to face with the question:

Who is on the throne?

Is it you, with your hurt and resentment? Or is it God, with His infinite compassion both for you and for the one who has trespassed against you?

As I write this, I realize that some of you may have known depths of suffering at the hands of others that I cannot even imagine. I have known enough to realize how hard this whole message is. To forgive another is not to condone what they have done; nor is it to negate what you feel. It is the Crucified One who calls you to forgive, and there is no compassion and no understanding in this universe greater than His. He knows every tear you have ever shed[5] and He knows the hurts too deep for tears. And He will avenge

---

5   Psalm 56:8

evil one day—but He will not allow bitterness to poison your heart. In God's eyes, it is far more pitiable to be the monster than to be the victim. No matter how badly you have been hurt, there is Life enough in Christ to restore you—to more than restore you.

God has loved you. God has forgiven you. He has laid His life down so that you may be free. Now go and be free in obedience; secure in His arms, close to His heart.

"Forgive us our debts, as we forgive our debtors"—and make us like You, God of our lives.

Delivered

"What then shall we say to these things? If God be for us, who can be against us? He that spared not his own Son, but delivered him up for us all, how shall he not with him freely give us all things?

"Who shall lay anything to the charge of God's elect? It is God that justifieth. Who is he that condemneth? It is Christ that died, yea rather, that is risen again, who is even at the right hand of God, who also maketh intercession for us.

"Who shall separate us from the love of Christ? shall tribulation, or distress, or persecution, or famine, or nakedness, or peril, or sword? Nay, in all these things we are more than conquerors through him that loved us.

"For I am persuaded, that neither death, nor life, nor angels, nor principalities, nor powers, nor things present, nor things to come, Nor height, nor depth, nor any other creature, shall be able to separate us from the love of God, which is in Christ Jesus our Lord."

THE APOSTLE PAUL
(Romans 8:31-35, 38-39)

DELIVER US FROM EVIL

*And lead us not into temptation,
but deliver us from evil.*

Lord, I sat with Your people yesterday. They laughed and joked about things You call abomination. They speak of righteousness like it's a straitjacket and sin like it's funny. Darkness clouds our eyes; we cannot see what truly is. If we truly saw sin, we would cry like David,

"There is no soundness in my flesh because of thine anger; neither is there any rest in my bones because of my sin. For mine iniquities are gone over my head: as an heavy burden they are too heavy for me. My wounds stink and are corrupt because of my foolishness. I am troubled; I am bowed down greatly; I go mourning all the day long. For my loins are filled with a loathsome disease:

and there is no soundness in my flesh. I am feeble and sore broken: I have roared by reason of the disquietness of my heart... For I am ready to halt, and my sorrow is continually before me. For I will declare mine iniquity; I will be sorry for my sin."[1]

Oh Lord, deliver us from evil.

Lord, someone misunderstood me yesterday. And up it came: all my self-righteousness like a towering idol, arms folded, eyes glaring; all my pride like a crawling worm, pretending humility; and anger—oh, how willing I was to believe evil of them! And someone else praised me highly, and how I preened. How I looked down on others; how I measured my actions so that everyone would see and think me good when all my motives were only for myself; oh, Lord, deliver me!

Deliver us from evil.

Lord, yesterday I put my duty up against my desires, and my desires won. I risked the well-being of others so I could have the petty thing I wanted. Yesterday I said I loved someone, and then I dishon-

---
1 Ps.38:3-8,17-18

oured that someone with my actions because I was busy impressing someone else.

*Lead us not into temptation,
but deliver us from evil.*

Lord, yesterday I read Your word with everyone else in mind. I preached instead of obeying. That wasn't all: I could have been gentle, and I destroyed. I knew the Truth: I told a lie. I should have praised, instead I worried. Yesterday it came down to me or You; it came down to obey or rebel; it came down to self or others. Lord... I'm sorry.

If I break my heart, will it make things better?

Deliver us from evil!

The Book says, "Overcome evil with good."[2] I'm not sure I understand, God.

Deliver us.

Lord, yesterday I read about "things that darken the sun." What I saw on the news... what I read in the history book...

---

2 Romans 12:21

what I heard people saying... oh God, deliver us! Are we all like this? All of us biting, scratching, clawing our way to the top in defiance of Right? Are we all so controlled by our desires? Can't we see what we're doing? Don't we care?

Oh God, I'm afraid. I'm afraid to walk down the street. I'm afraid of the future. I'm afraid of people. I'm afraid of myself. I'm afraid of Satan, of the next Hitler, of disaster, of death, of temptation, of government, of fear itself.

Deliver us from evil.

Lord, yesterday I heard the people screaming. I saw the twisted faces; I saw the grasping hands and the empty souls. Yesterday I heard them making choices:

Jesus or Barabbas?

They chose Death; they condemned Life.

Guilt or innocence?

They didn't care what guilt there was, only that it seemed to be in their best interest to kill Him. If I wash my hands of this, will it make things better?

Courage or cowardice?

Judas betrayed Him; Peter denied Him.

The others scattered.

Yesterday I heard the people mocking; yesterday I heard the whips beating; yesterday I heard the demons laughing; yesterday I heard the hammer fall. Yesterday I heard Him cry out "Why?" and there was no answer.

I waited for the words He did not say. I waited for Him to lash out. I waited for Him to scream, to claw, to climb over others and push His way to the top.

He didn't do it.

I waited for the rebellion. He didn't rebel. He didn't even open His mouth to defend Himself.

He said, "Father, forgive them." He won. He overcame evil with good.

> *Crucified. Beaten, mocked, accused, abandoned, forsaken, crucified.*
>
> *Delivered...*
>
> *We are delivered.*

"Knowing this, that our old man is crucified with him, that the body of sin might be destroyed, that henceforth we should not serve sin. For he that is dead is freed from sin... For in that he died, he died unto sin once: but in that he liveth, he liveth unto

God.

"Likewise reckon ye also yourselves to be dead indeed unto sin, but alive unto God through Jesus Christ our Lord."[3]

You have delivered us from evil.

Lord, yesterday it came down to me or You; it came down to obey or rebel; it came down to self or others. I felt it all in me: biting, clawing, scratching its way to the surface. But You are also in me: I cried out for deliverance. I believed. I obeyed.

And I am delivered from evil.

---

[3] Romans 6:6-7, 10-11

The Hymn of Creation

*Praise the L*ORD *from the earth,*
ye dragons, and all deeps:

Fire, and hail; snow, and vapour;
stormy wind fulfilling his word:

Mountains, and all hills; fruit-
ful trees, and all cedars:

Beasts, and all cattle; creep-
ing things, and flying fowl:

Kings of the earth, and all people: princ-
es, and all judges of the earth:

Both young men, and maid-
ens; old men, and children:

*Let them praise the name of the L*ORD*:*
for his name alone is excellent; his glo-
ry is above the earth and heaven.

Hallelujah.

PSALM 148:7-13

THINE IS

For thine is the kingdom,
and the power,
and the glory, for ever.
Amen

Humble God dressed like a man; Righteous Man speaking like a God.

We were meant to worship worthiness, hallow holiness, and follow greatness to the death. Open our eyes and ears and hearts to know in You the One King above all gods.

Exalted Lord washing feet like a servant; Eternal Servant claiming our allegiance. To you all loyalty is owed. We shall worship through calm and tempest; we shall trust You in darkness and light; we shall live our lives last so that You may be first. In Your reign, in Your rule, we shall bring every strain into the Song of Love, and the earth shall be filled with the knowledge of God as the waters cover the sea.

For Thine is the Kingdom.

Judge and Forgiver; Death's Victim and Destroyer; once Forsaken, now Free. You are the Man who brings Creation to its knees.

Your voice is heard in the thunder. Your voice in the wind. Your hand pulls down the wicked, Your hand lifts up the poor.

You make the stars burn and the earth turn, send the rain and call forth the flowers. Your finger once etched Law in stone; now writes righteousness on our hearts. You save the chief of sinners, turn mourning into dancing, give us joy for ashes. You make the broken whole again. You make the human holy, make the faithless faithful, make the wicked righteous, and set the captive free.

For Thine is the Power.

The voices of the seas lift to You; the light of the sun shines for You. For You the flowers bloom and the righteous prosper. In our love we love You; in our humility we exalt You; in our triumphs we extol You; in our hearts we worship.

Emotion, strong and passionate, quiet and lovely, bears witness to You. Righteousness, walked out every day; right choices, gentle triumphs, overcoming, forbearing, loving, trusting, all for You. All bear witness to You, all exalt You, all proclaim that You are and You are Beautiful. We proclaim that You are All in All.

For Thine is the Glory.

Forever and ever.

Amen.

VISIT

www.littledozen.com

FOR

Devotional Articles

Free eBooks and Exciting Fiction

Writing Tips

Church and Family Resources

Information on Upcoming Titles

Blogs

More

Visit Inklings,
the blog of Rachel Starr Thomson
http://rachelstarrthomson.blogspot.com

Did You Enjoy This Book?

Do you know someone who would benefit by reading it? SPREAD THE WORD! As a small press, we value the power of READERS to decide what is worth reading. We believe that a book's true value cannot be measured in marketing dollars. The worth of a book is in the impact it has on YOUR life. If you have seen value in this book, we encourage you to let others know.

IT'S SIMPLE:

- Spread the word!
- Give a copy as a gift.
- Leave a review on Amazon.com or BarnesandNoble.com. Then email us a copy so we can post in on LittleDozen.com.
- If you write a newsletter, ezine, blog, or print column, consider letting your readers know about this book!
- Send us an email to let us know how much this book has touched you: publisher@littledozen.com

Contribute to the work of Bible translation worldwide: 15% of every purchase of Heart to Heart made through the publisher's Web site is donated to Wycliffe Bible Translators!

Praise for Letters to a Samuel Generation

"I have really appreciated your Letters to a Samuel Generation. It's been a blessing to be able to include them in our publications to inspire our younger (and older) readers. I appreciate how you are able to keep a balance in building faith, yet acknowledging pain. Calling to action, yet reminding people that BEing comes out of doing. And calling for unity, while still stressing the need to stand for truth."

 - Mercy Hope, regular columnist for An Encouraging Word Magazine, and interviewer for FaithTalks.com

"I recently read your article entitled 'Beauty' in the Home School Digest magazine. As my mom commented, the writing and message were 'beautiful' (pun intended). I found it very encouraging that people exist who realize the departure of true Godly beauty from our arts, society, and lives. It also inspired me to be one who, with God's strength, shines to the world HIS beauty."

 - Aaron Dodson, age 19, Remnant Productions

"Just a note to say that I really enjoyed this month's ezine.....to your description of what God's practical love is, my spirit shouted a resounding 'yes!' "

 - Robin Gilman, homeschooling mother of 10

Coming Soon
FROM LITTLE DOZEN PRESS

Letters to a Samuel Generation: The Collection

by Rachel Starr Thomson

Each chapter of Heart to Heart: Meeting With God in the Lord's Prayer was originally published as part of an online ezine called Letters to a Samuel Generation.

Now available as a hardbound book from Little Dozen Press, Letters has encouraged believers all over the world, from teenagers to missionaries to mothers and pastors.

Available March 2007 from LittleDozen.com, Amazon.com, and other online retailers, or special order from your local bookstore.

www.ingramcontent.com/pod-product-compliance
Lightning Source LLC
Chambersburg PA
CBHW031259290426
44109CB00012B/649